NOT VANISHING

NOT VANISHING

CHRYSTOS

PRESS GANG PUBLISHERS
VANCOUVER

Canadian Cataloguing in Publication Data

Chrystos, 1946–
    Not vanishing

    Poems.
    ISBN 0-88974-015-1

    I. Title.
    PS3553.H57N6   1988   811'.54   C88-091260-X

Earlier versions of some of the poems in this book have appeared in *This Bridge Called My Back, A Gathering of Spirit, Sinister Wisdom, Conditions, Sapphic Touch, WomanSpirit, Sunbury* and *Plexus*.

Feather drawings and Four Directions symbol on the cover painted by Chrystos.

First printing May, 1988   Second printing August, 1988

Designed and typeset by Penny Goldsmith in Bembo and Aldus. Type produced by The Typeworks.
Cover and book layout by Val Speidel.
Editor for the Press: Barbara Kuhne.
Printed by the collective labour of Press Gang Printers.
Bound in Canada

Press Gang Publishers
603 Powell Street
Vancouver, B.C. V6A 1H2   Canada

Because there are so many myths & misconceptions about Native people, it is important to clarify myself to the reader who does not know me. I was not born on the reservation, but in San Francisco, part of a group called "Urban Indians" by the government. I grew up around Black, Latin, Asian & white people & am shaped by that experience, as well as by what my father taught me. He had been taught to be ashamed & has never spoken our language to me. Much of the fury which erupts from my work is a result of seeing the pain that white culture has caused my father. It continues to give pain to all of us. I am not the "Voice" of Native women, nor representative of Native women in general. I am not a "Spiritual Leader," although many white women have tried to push me into that role. While I am deeply spiritual, to share this with strangers would be a violation. Our rituals, stories & religious practices have been stolen & abused, as has our land. I don't publish work which would encourage this—so you will find no creation myths here. My purpose is to make it as clear & as inescapable as possible, what the actual, material conditions of our lives are. Hunger, infant mortality, forced sterilization, treaty violations, the plague of alcohol & drugs, ridiculous jail terms, denial of civil rights, radiation poisoning, land theft, endless contrived legal battles which drain our wills, corrupt "tribal" governments, harassment & death at the hands of the BIA & FBI are the realities we face. Don't admire what you perceive as our stoicism or spirituality—work for our lives to continue in our own Ways. Despite the books which still appear, even in radical bookstores, we are not Vanishing Americans.

This book is for all Native Women

especially for Barbara Cameron, Sharol Graves, Kim Anno, Anita
Valerio, Jo Carrillo, Burning Cloud, Gloria Anzaldúa, Beth Brant,
Leota LoneDog, Celeste George, Dian Million, Elizabeth Woody,
Lillian Pitt, Karen Timentwa, Amanda White, Viv Haskell, Jackie
Davenport, Maria Williams, Jeannette Allen, Marsha Gomez, Paula
Gunn Allen, Joy Harjo, Vickie Sears, Dee Johnson, Janet McCloud,
Chris Stewart, Bonnie Price, Raven & Sipsus in Maine, who gave me
a turtle story to carry me through

and for our future in

Rebecca, Manley, Kyle, Scott, Stephanie, Jim, Juanita, Sherri, Pajuta,
Jamie Lee, Rashida, Tatsu, Ahmad, Rubin, Cassie & Afi Loren

CONTENTS

The work is arranged in roughly chronological order, in the pace of one of my readings.

CRAZY GRANDPA WHISPERS

tells me: take a pick ax to new car row   hack & clear the land
    plant Hopi corn down to the sea
tells me: break open that zoo buffalo corral
    chase them snorting through the streets
tells me: put up tipis in every vacant lot
    shelter the poor without rent
tells me: steal those dogs the pound suffocates
    cook them for Lakota stew
    feed the hungry without words
Crazy grandpa supposed to be dead   They locked him up
He withered   Not dead I feel him shrivel against my backbone
    when I see anybody behind bars
Grandpa tells me: take back these cities
    live as your ancestors   Sew up the mouths of the enemy
    with their damn beads
Grandpa I hear you through walls of my skin
Grandpa if I obey you they'll lock me up again
    like they did you
        Grandpa it's such a fine
fine line
    between my instincts & their sanity laws
    I've no time to sew moccasins
        Grandpa I'm still learning how to walk in this world
        without getting caught

YOU CAN'T GET GOOD HELP THESE DAZE

Hey   Hey   Mrs. Robinson I'm keeping
your toenails & hair
I've got plans for you
as I scrub your French Blue bathroom floor hands & knees
stinking of Parson's sudsy ammonia   empty your wastebaskets
Iron your daughter's overalls & t-shirts
Polish your silver trays   tea sets   compotes   spoons
& furniture   Listen   I want a trust fund too
I'm as intimate as your daughter   don't I know
your husband's pubic hair   his piss outside the bowl
Mrs. Robinson I'm as close
to you as anybody gets to anyone else
Ironing your hand-embroidered cherry sprig slips
amber linen breakfast napkins   emptying pink tampon tubes
Mrs. Robinson I know   about you   Your whole life
sits in green flowered easy chairs I dust
I have an interest   in some
of the money you've got in yellow page bank books
I plan to get more out of you   than $21.50 a week
Mrs. Robinson I'm already amusing myself
studying your schedule   figuring the locks   watching
for burglar alarm wires as I vacuum so intently your doe
velvet carpets   I don't want your little trinkets
things you're afraid I might steal   No   you can trust me
you're glad   feel safe
I've no desire to take your collections home
where I'd still   be polishing them   Mrs. Robinson
I'm scheming   busy with your toenails   making
plans for you   & for me   I think
I'll be willing to settle
for 300 thousand

FOOLISH

I dance   hoot   holler   coo

LOOK   these clouds   these blue blue skies full of deer

Japanese flowering quince winks me a rosy morning

We're beginning!   First time   arrives with yellow smells

surprises   These friends I planted   rise up to embrace me

All the people are buds

their hearts whisper cream   blue   purple

Time for us to come forward with green lips

Peas sprout!   Corn whinnies!   Squash rumbles!

Here we come   *Here we come*   *Get ready to*

know us   *Throw your doors down*

Here come spiders   lambs with round bellies & long legs

Let's drink these red throats of song

LOOK   this is the moon of opens wide

this is the moon of wind who plays

this is the moon of rain & sun together

UNFOLD YOUR LEAVES NOW

we begin

ACCIDENT

Windshield meets my face   cracks   inside prism shattered
a lap full of diamonds   dribble off my shoulders   Hot
copper taste of blood   thick   chokes   swallow it   Eyelashes
webbed shut   I'm upsidedown   no   I'm here   repeating birth
through glass   tumble of legs   arms fly off   sun cooks
my blood   Lip split   bathe it with my tongue   want to heal
some part which now belongs to cries of hospital corridors
Watched him hit   us   stared into his face   what
was he doing   skidded three car lengths before he stopped   Didn't
speak red light language   Had a large car   an American nightmare
of a car   we were in Hitler's beetle   I was the main line
intersection of impact   day's entertainment at the corner
of Shattuck & Dwight   My bleeding disorder leaves steaming pools
Want it back   Don't leave my blood on the black street   Give
me a word for pain that's sharp enough   Stains up through
my jeans   coming under the thin blue threads   blood falls
on top of seeping blood in my ears   Teeth stuck together with terror
My arms hold bouquet of glass knives   Everything sparkles red
landscape cut by blood red fire engine   I'm trapped   the door
caved in sucks my breasts   Truck sprouts men in black rain coats
carrying a torch   they'll blast me out with flames   Red tongues
chew through deep blue metal   scream   they're trying to blow up
my feet   fear eats me   a deep ice red wail   Sky smeared as
the sun goes down   as they lift the door away like a wing
shovel me into a narrow white shaft   strap me into backbone
stare at ambulance ceiling pale sick room green   smooth metal
ridges   I need the cool blue distance of clouds   He puts that
black rubber explosion on my arm   *Keep breathing* he says   *Stay
awake*   Watches me closely this stranger with no right to my face
an intimate second   our eyes collide   I see by the way he
twitches away from me that my eyes are glittering black broken pain
He checks my pulse again   his starched white uniform marred
by dark blue bruises near the pocket which holds his pen   His
hands glint with hair   I'm black & out

4

New & improved the emergency room chews me with plastic
disposable gadgets   gowns which snap   Old this smell of fear in
my armpits   Not sterile in this white place my body feels the shock
abandoned red as blood the door screams open   I tunnel under thin
blankets certain I'll be misplaced   My fingers carve the sheets
I'm a woman not an accident   no one is listening   Suddenly
I'm missing   have to return   slide through the roof
to the source   see the hole in the crash   doesn't have my voice
split angry in hard shriek   I drum the man who tried to drive
through us into a blue battered heap   I rip out his spine   he who
walked away   he who lied/told the cop that he had the right of way
the green light   he whose wife in fur coat screamed at me as I
was carried away   I fill up my lost red animals with my throat
crying blue   leave this howl in the street   bristling

O HONEYSUCKLE WOMAN

won't you lay with me
our tongues flowering
open-throated
golden pollen
We could drink one another
sticky sweet & deep
our bodies tracing silver snail trails
Our white teeth nibbling
We could swallow desire whole
fingers caught in our sweet smell
We'd transform the air
O honey woman
won't you suckle me
Suckling
won't you let me
honey you

for Nanci Stern

I WALK IN THE HISTORY OF MY PEOPLE

There are women locked in my joints
    for refusing to speak to the police
My red blood full of those
    arrested   in flight   shot
My tendons stretched brittle with anger
    do not look like white roots of peace
In my marrow are hungry faces
    who live on land the whites don't want
In my marrow women who walk 5 miles every day for water
In my marrow the swollen hands of my people who are not allowed
    to hunt
    to move
    to be
In the scars of my knees you can see
    children torn from their families
    bludgeoned into government schools
You can see through the pins in my bones
    that we are prisoners of a long war
My knee is so badly wounded no one will look at it
The pus of the past oozes from every pore
This infection has gone on for at least 300 years
    Our sacred beliefs have been made into pencils
    names of cities   gas stations
My knee is wounded so badly that I limp constantly
    Anger is my crutch   I hold myself upright with it
        My knee is wounded
            see
                How I Am Still Walking

DOCTOR'S FAVORITE COLOR

Her office blue enough to break you   accusations in her indigo
velvet throw pillows   her coarse royal blue hopsacking couch
her teal tweed carpeting where hours of my mind unreeled without
catching anything   She bought paintings of misty
flowers which evaporated in a delicate smoke of wounds   Wouldn't
hang mine which leaned ashamed in her coat closet   Innocent
robin's egg blue walls condensed at a slate blue metal
desk containing alphabetical files of our nightmares   her extra
nylon stockings & fastidious letterhead   Crane's best rag
pale blue kid finish with navy engraving   Those windows watched
the bay where we'd waited for my father on rough docks
when he left   left again   left
Somewhere else we waved a white tablecloth to him over sharp
bridge railings   his dark ant body far below on deck   passing
under us   the wind beat my coat through my knees blue with cold
I stared out her mirrors   my father floated in every ship
as he listened to the complaints of officers in white duckskin
     gold braid snakes   She wanted me to re-enact what I couldn't
feel   handed me Fisher Price toy dolls to show her what it
was like when my uncle took off my flannel pajamas to make
me a real woman at 12   I explained my mother   hours
of her voice repeated in mine while the baby blue
telephone silently blinked for help   Doctor A told me being
Indian didn't matter   Said I had Character Psychosis
Doctor A she had her nose carved down   changed her last name
joined the Unity Church   wore blue contact lenses   dyed
her hair blonde as can be   carefully denied her Jewish father
My visions   she assured me   were part of my sickness
a tunnel my eyes couldn't light   So busy being not
who she was born   how could she see me   as her desperately
thalo blue curtains kept their stiff folds   She listened   bent
forward on her Prussian blue velvet chair   to eat with her eyes
the rose I saw glistening in multi-colored radiance on her exit
door   Cheeks cold with confusion I touched nothing
The state sent her forms in triplicate white pink & blue
which cured me at their expense   She said I lived as though
I had no skin   my heart hemophiliac   waited when she was late
with the tear-streaked patient ahead of me   Shivered

her door opened   she leaned with a smile   *Come On In*
Blue birds of happiness wheeled in her teeth   my stomach
empty   her voice cooed   *How Are We Today*
inferring a relationship I didn't swallow   Her sympathy
like cheap perfume in a crowded elevator   I had no room
for her explanations of my overdoses   Drugs she ordered
that boiled me in passivity   Her thin unwatered
philodendron whose brown strangling roots revoked my life
laid me out in double solitaire with a taste of antiseptic
Moans through her black leather padded door   Scuttle
of metal instruments in the sterilizer of the office down
the hall   My breath held itself   against time clicking
her turquoise clock in random mockery   I didn't tell her
the trouble was   I wouldn't live
if I was a chronic undifferentiated schizophrenic thing
my skin apostasy   Her room aborted   Her voice pulled
me through azure walls   I was open to stars & coyote howls
She suggested I go to the day care center
where we danced in a circle with scarves
trying to be planets rotating around the sun
or strung wooden beads with dull awls   or accepted
paper cups of yellow & blue pills at the end
of long silent lines   She committed
me   times when I didn't   make sense   to her
dangerous mystery   I was so quiet & so loud   Cadet blue
she had no smell   dry as anesthesia my throat couldn't swallow
her face   I was acid–etched in a red sky   She was nowhere
in sight   as she spoke   said she wanted
                    to help me

in honor of Sheila Gilhooly

SAILING

in a boat of brambles our lips ripe
Our purple tongues signal the full moon
in hot metaphors
Your long fingers slip
the sweetest berries into my mouth
I drink your juiciness
Rowing with soft strokes we
bring one another home
Plant a future out of season
I promise pies
You promise plenty of fruit   .

for Pat

THERE IS A MAN WITHOUT FINGERPRINTS

who tortures   rapes   murders
Three of us have grown cold under him in six months
The police are testing his semen scraped out
      of our dead vaginas   They have no clues
He attacks with a nylon stocking right inside the door
Those keys dangling from our locks don't speak his name
in the morning   He uses our kitchen knives   wearing gloves
to keep his hands clean
He tortured one of us for eight hours before her death
The coroner knows these things with the precision of our terror
            We shows signs of defending ourselves
cut palms   bruised knuckles   He thinks the barrio
is his territory   All of the women lived alone
I live alone   holding a knife of murder in my stomach ready for him
I watch the street as I come home with razor eyes ready for him
I kick open my door ready for him
He attacks between 8 and 10 at night   Knew the habits
of the women he's killed   Watching us
from coffee shop windows in cool sips
The police   who don't like to be called pigs
are keeping him under wraps   They say
they don't want us to panic
I only know about him   because a woman police dispatcher
announced him in my History Of Women class
Her words a morgue
This is not a poem   it's a newspaper   a warning written quickly
Always be on guard   ready to kill   to survive
He has no face   He could be   any man
watching you

FOR SHAROL GRAVES

Deep breath   Inhale the drums   Feet begin
We sway in fringed shawls
sparkling beadwork   deerskin leggings
to the voice of the South Drum singing
gently tin cones tingle   Whispers of women
as we wheel around the sun
wearing jewel-colored velvet skirts
moccasins only for dancing
holding eagle feather fans   family blankets
Beyond us   the men leap & prance shaking bells
their roaches bob
We're a circle apart
within
First time you and I have danced together
In the distance
big silver cans steam with stew
drunks reel
children eat fry bread dripping with honey & butter
Our feet pass over the earth with soft thuds
Your otter fur braids swish
You've worked all year
on the Thunderbird belt & ribbonwork skirt
for this day
Your beauty echoes
beyond drums
Holds me
here now in my kitchen as I remember
dancing with you washed in light
Our spirits whirl
Step into
the still center
of a friendship drum

MAYBE WE SHOULDN'T MEET
IF THERE ARE NO THIRD WORLD WOMEN HERE

My mouth cracks in familiar shock   my eyes flee
to the other faces where my rage desperation fear pain ricochet
a thin red scream   How can you miss our brown & golden
in this sea of pink   We're not as many as you
But we're here   You're the ones who called a community
meeting & didn't contact the Black Lesbians or G.A.L.A. or
Gay American Indians or the Disabled Women's Coalition or
Gay Asians or anyone I know
You're the ones who don't print your signs in Spanish or Chinese
or any way but how you talk   You're the ones standing three
feet away from a Black woman saying
There are no Third World women here
Do you think we are Martians
All those workshops on racism won't help you open your eyes & see
how you don't even see us
How can we come to your meetings if we are invisible
Don't look at me with guilt   Don't apologize   Don't struggle
with the problem of racism like algebra
Don't write a paper on it for me to read or hold a meeting in
which you discuss what to do to get us to come to your
time & your place
We're not your problems to understand & trivialize
We don't line up in your filing cabinets under "R" for rights
Don't make the racist assumption that the issue of racism
between us
is yours   at me
Bitter boiling I can't see you

CLOSE YOUR EYES

Come
into a deep dark flower   night woman   inside
crescent moon petals   Scratch your back on this magenta
Roll around in scarlet   Wake Up   Open fur lips
eat your saffron supper   Lick her   Tongues in your fingers
taste her midnight bloom with thirsty skin
Hold her petals of teal   lime   russet   silver
white light gold grass on a summer sleeping hill
stroke this blue gray cradle   These petal colors of dreamtime
realtime in her hidden flower   Here!   Listen!   Now melts
Take off your think about it clothes
Leave your answers in the closet
Come for her petals glowing   eyes open along your arms
in this place   her secret mouth   her planting smell   We'll wet
these snow petals   pale peach petals
early morning lavender petals
See her in the deep holding time   floating colortime
coming hometime   Climb into her silver melon breast
held in the noplace of petals   Downy
Here's a dance singing
here's a place to gurgle   laugh   sucking
warm sweet   sweet   in her curly midnight flower
Lotus of a thousand skies   Each color an opening
your eyes lick her
sun yellow   moon blue   pine green   sunrise pink
into her night flower   her moon bloom
inside her dark fur corolla
Roll yourself wet
red   salmon   sepia   mud brown   violet   gold
Paint your mouth in petals
Stay

DANCE A GHOST

Thump I leap you   shake

    down memories   your black wings

  in my throat   hoarse   You die, are buried

your name closes the door

        you reappear at night   eyes wide   I see the uncaught

white man his shoes polished his hand gun

    last pulse   the heart contracts   dreams your knees crumple

    red neon flickers over your redman hands

    black moccasins on white ground

      curl unseen without frame

No bells on your feet   feathers still   soles

    worn through

    I dance you

for Mani, murdered with his friend Marcus outside a Phoenix bar

15

KUAN YIN   GODDESS OF MERCY

writes to Francis of Assisi
explains the meaning of light   water   understanding
Many birds are in her words
She says she misses him   Asks when she may visit again
& how are his Chinese conversation studies progressing
Theirs is a special relationship she says   Not easily
understood by many   including themselves but their long silences
are not indifference
On the contrary   he is one of her best pupils
His eyes clear very quickly
She is sure the light on water will speak to him soon

They say   *He's babbling that nonsense again*
because he forgets where he is   speaks Chinese
He sees her face in everyone

She grows impatient when he does not reply
turns her eyes elsewhere
He suffers visions of hell

He writes to ask her if she will come
Too late   She's found
another
whose constancy reflects light
He speaks Chinese to the birds

for Anita Taylor Oñang

16

TODAY WAS A BAD DAY LIKE TB

Saw whites clap during a sacred dance
Saw young blond hippie boy with a red stone pipe
    My eyes burned him up
He smiled   *This is a Sioux pipe* he said from his sportscar
    Yes   I hiss   *I'm wondering how you got it*
    & the name is Lakota not Sioux
I'll tell you he said all friendly & liberal as only
    those with no pain can be
    I turned away   Can't charm me   can't bear to know
thinking of the medicine bundle I saw opened up in a glass case
    with a small white card beside it
    naming the rich whites who say they
    "own" it
Maybe they have an old Indian grandma back in time
    to excuse themselves
Today was a day I wanted to beat up the smirking man wearing
a pack with a Haida design from Moe's bookstore
Listen Moe's   How many Indians do you have working there?
How much money are you sending the Haida people
to use their sacred Raven design?
    You probably have an Indian grandma too
    whose name you don't know
    Today was a day like TB
    you cough & cough trying to get it out
        all that comes
            is blood & spit

for Amanda White

POEM FOR LETTUCE

I know
you don't want to be eaten
anymore than a cow or a pig or a chicken does
but   they're the vicious vegetarians
& they say you do
Gobbling up the innocent green beings who gladden
any reasonable person's heart
    I'll tell you little lettuce
you'll see them in cowskin shoes & belts
    & nobody can make sense of that
Those virtuous vegetarians they'll look at you with prim distaste
    while you enjoy your bacon
        Makes me want
to buy some cowboy movie blood capsules
    Imagine an introduction
I'd like you to meet Lily, she's a non-smoking non-drinking
vegetarian separatist Pisces with choco-phobia
& I smile
while secretly biting down on the capsules concealed in my cheeks
    then shake her hand   drooling blood
I whisper
Hi   I'm a flaming carnivorous double Scorpio who'll eat anything
& as she wilts in dismay   trembles with trepidation
hisses with disgust
Ah   then   little lettuces
    we'll have our moment of laughing revenge

for Elizabeth Markell

18

THE SILVER WINDOW

tells me I'm a thick & simple woman whose hands
have washed many plates   cups   bowls
says my hair is a long
dark sweep knotted in a past I don't sing
Eyes deep as the earth I turn over for squash & peas
my face a map of disease survived
my skin has followed the sun
to a rainy place where a blue heron nests silently
The silver window tells a story of who I am when others look
you could easily see that I fold the clothes & sweep the floor
for a living   A face of the plains my family crossed
one that echoes wild rice   elk
traded corn from the place of light
The silver window covers my memories like snow
melted in a day
They say I dance behind
a silver window could say so   but I'll tell you
this morning   I rose
from dreams
a slow moving lake deep with fish
many birds in the grasses   this morning
the silver window was blank with my beauty   I came
with the sun
burning off mist
I sang all the way
to the bottom

for Jo Carrillo

MY BABY BROTHER

rides a blank face snow pony
same one I rode
through rat alleys   garbage halls   crash pads   screw johns
jack it up
　　3 times he's come to stay with me
& kick
all 3   my rent went up his arm
that cool dead horse   that rocking down to smooth snow nothing
horse   kills the pain of a white fence world   hard walls world
eat or be eaten cement world
kills me to see his eyes like marbles   his arms a map of war
his heart so faint a drum
My baby brother rides a death head white powder stony horse
　　　　　somewhere
　　　　　last heard of in Texas
　　　　　a year ago

VISION : BUNDLE

within   mystery wrapped in torn deer hide
 We cannot speak of the sacred
Our mother is who they want to strip : pull out her bones
 fuel their air conditioners
 unconditioned air is the one
  we breathe
  speaks to us
tongues of stars   wind   times to plant   times to be silent
They have a machine for everything   even this
one soul looking for a song we might dream
a smooth place where we could dance together
 without separation
Buttons push them
We live trapped in places we can't dig out of or move
 walls hold old voices
want to be taken down & aired   Go to a new place
No one speaks our languages
My father is ashamed of
My mother won't think
We've dead relatives & friends with no common burial place
 Scattered   they say we are vanishing
 leaves of autumn   red dust raked away so the snow can fall flat
They have our bundles split open in museums
 our dresses & shirts at auctions
 our languages on tape
 our stories in locked rare book libraries
 our dances on film
The only part of us they can't steal
   is what we know

for Barbara Cameron

21

YESTERDAY HE CALLED HER A PIG

he's a white man/she's Black

she's his boss/he was egged on by some politically correct

white lesbians

it's better to avoid the subject of colors

Today I swept her floor   washed her sheets

cleaned her kitchen   bought food

arranged a bouquet of bright

red carnations

I love her   want to be an eraser for her

Bear her insult   more insults

I let in light

put her books in a careful stack beside the bed

brought flowers

it didn't help

for Valerie Street

WOMAN

will you come with me moving
through rivers to soft lakebeds
Come gathering wild rice with sticks
will you go with me
down the long waters smoothly shaking
life into our journey
Will you bring this gift with me
We'll ask my brother to dance on it
until the wildness sings

for Leota LoneDog

MEDITATION FOR GLORIA ANZALDÚA

On my forehead a bird in flight
going places I can't see
feathered in light my whole body aches
& pulls following a tide
Moon has become my lover
lulls me with phosphorescent hands
Her hair tangles mine like roots
As far as my heart reaches   water breathes   silver fish
swimming in my fingers to food of colors
Each stone in my shoe a reminder that I've so little time
beauty is
so vast   I've so much more to get away with
before there is no more
with a hunger like fat red buds on brambles etched in frost
hunger like winter mallards combing breakers for life   hunger
that burns me   infernos   hungry for early spring waiting
in earth   hungry for a shape I alone can make
Wanting to blend water & fire
Paint a deeper surface where
we surge
I want to take our breath away
like this eagle diving for a shrew
I want to go where all
the wings are

MAMA WANTS ME TO COME

home for Christmas
Better Homes & Gardens says daughter is supposed
to show up smiling   Pretend it's not old cans
    bottles   yellow newspapers
I come to your vacant lot   put a teacup on my knee
    watch you try to drape my queerness in ruffles
    stare at the dried weeds of memory
We've nothing   in common
different views of the same demolishing crew
    Your words are rubble mama   broken bricks
glass shards   rats   dog shit
    I come home like a wino falls asleep in a doorway
I come like fitting in a space no one else wants
    Your vacant eyes are weeping
want me to say I love you & I do
but I've rented a room with no view
        I burn your letter
            to keep warm

NO PUBLIC SAFETY

I can't tell you how much
they want to lock her up
She sleeps in their building   It's trespassing   How would you
like to come to work in the morning & have to step over her
See how little she has   compared to you
Chronic Paranoid Schizophrenic they say
The law is ambiguous   Can she take care of herself
or not
Obviously not if she thinks the building for Public Safety
means just that
There are laws against the literal interpretation of words
She has been taken to Western State Hospital & observed
They say she hallucinates
Join the army   murder a lot of people you don't know   but don't
hallucinate   That's crazy
Incompetent to stand trial they say   Would you
let her live in your house   sleep on your porch
keep her bags in your garage   pitch a tipi for her on your lawn
What would the neighbors think
Better lock her up   We don't want to look at failure   scares us
isn't safe   They say for her to sleep alone in that building
why anything could happen to her
Let's keep the building warm & lit all night even after
the janitors go home   We like to take better care
of our papers   file cabinets   metal desks   plastic chairs
potted plants   posters of trees in Yosemite
than an old woman
Who does she think she is anyway   expecting us to help
to give her safety   Anyone who doesn't take care of themselves
should be locked up   we have lots of places for it
We're all terrified   not of growing old   but of being unable
to take care of ourselves
Would you rather sleep in the Public Safety Building
or be locked up on a back ward at Western State Hospital
the food   the drugs   regular & terrible
This is her second trial   Keep the lawyers off the streets
They can take care of themselves with a little help
from their wives who clean   buy groceries   take the suits

to the cleaners   change the bed   cook meals   raise
the children   & admire
Who admires Anna Mae Peoples besides me
What is shelter   the judge asks rhetorically
you won't catch HIM sleeping under bridges or begging
$40,230 buys a lot of shelter   a king size bed
hot massage shower   wall to wall carpeting or probably
oriental rugs   A long time ago Anna Mae Peoples
probably waxed judges' floors
Too old now her back hurts all the time
the cool floor of the Public Safety Building is all she asks
They want to label her gravely disabled
they think there's a very good chance they'll win
Nowhere in the six column article
is one word
that Anna Mae Peoples has to say

for Anna Mae Peoples

GREEN

bright curve of snake
slides through spring fallen pink petals
in the lime grass
going someplace with a smooth slither sleek
move along   move along says her head
eyes black as night & more
Faster
than writing this

ANITA TAYLOR OÑANG

April 23, 1951 —February 24, 1986

Cry to the sun on a pearl rainy day singing blues arms full
of flowers   she has terminal cancer
at 34
Try to read an old cookbook at breakfast   brie & crackers
anything to forget   a recipe for mulled claret
one for witches' coffee
ladled from a silver bowl full of brandy & flames
Her face is on this page   Her eyes speak of always home
She loves to fish   See   her bend intently over water
reflections wavering gently on her brown rich skin
her black hair glowing   wispy   long   caught back
but not really   Her laugh   O wide & taking everyone in
How can we keep going without her smile   Corny   Beloved corn
gift I can no longer bring as she waits in morphine for her sister
to arrive from Germany where she fled after
the Rajneesh explosion   Detained by the US Government
she may not be able to come in time   for last words
Time   We rage at pink tape   a handy target for what belongs
to something we have no name for which takes Anita/leaves Marcos
She doesn't fit in here
Her calligraphy dances right past our eyes   butterflies
in her wake   Could I tell you of her lovely delicate rooms
which appeared & disappeared as she moved in three months or ten
Flowers   embroidered cloths   tea cups   A buddha with fat red
candles flickering as we spoke in half sentences of our
spiritual journeys   brushing the place lightly as wings
our words   dust in sunlight   against death
Her life gives me so much   As she swims toward peace
selfish I want to drag her back shouting   *This is not possible*
hooking it in my throat   too harsh a weight on her flight
Time   for this pain   ours   when we've seen her through
singing   O   crying to the sun

I'M MAKING YOU UP

Grandma we all need
partially deaf & busy with weaving
     listens   through a thick blanket of years & sore feet
nods   while I cry about everything they did to me
how horrible   & can't stand another
while brown wrinkled you smile at me like sun coming up
     I stand next to you   pass wool absently
       you lay aside the wrong colors   without comment
I'm simply   Grandchild
babbling   your sympathy warm & comforting as dust
     I sit in your lap   your loom pushed aside
you feed me fry bread with too much maple syrup
     I pull your braids   you cradle me deeper in
       your legs folded to make a basket for me
Grandma   who died long before I was born
                    Come Back
                         Come Back

for Beth Brant

30

YOUR DEPARTURE

is a hard spoon caught

throat dry   hands numb   bad headache

still with longing   no words no tears   careful

to comb hair   eat scrambled eggs with a dull fork

Take keys   turn on windshield wipers   drive slowly

Muted noise   chattering birds fly across your leaving air

quick brilliance of scotch broom continues

as when you arrived a week ago with wet darting tongue

dreamt me awake & more   I want you to stay/you can't

I watch you drink coffee with cream   staring out the window

your arriving airplane a silver knife

for Leota LoneDog

PORTRAIT OF ASSIMILATION

My father sits quietly in his brown Naugahyde chair watching
    TV with the remote control
    held out in his hand
He switches off the sound
at the commercials   while intently gazing at the picture
    His hair is cut short
he wears an electronic watch, white shirt, brown tie, gray sweater
carefully polished black leather shoes
Under his feet a prairie of green gold wall to wall carpet
says nothing
His chair is placed to hide the bad crack in the wall
& to catch the heat from an economy quartz unit
The walls are covered with paintings by his children
    photographs of his grandchildren
A yellow box of Kleenex is on the table near a carved tusk
    made to look like a fish   & a coral rose   he grew
in a turquoise glass vase from Woolworth's
          The way you know
           it's really him
is the way he's wrapped
          old style
          in a red & blue blanket
He says
          Gets kinda cold nowadays for me

for Canyon Sam

32

Gift: Seagull   Chrytos/1978

WINGS OF A WILD GOOSE

A hen, one who could have brought more geese, a female, a wild one
dead   Shot by an excited ignorant young blond boy, his first
His mother threw the wings in the garbage   I rinsed them
brought them home, hung them spread wide on my studio wall
A reminder of so much, saving what I can't bear to be wasted
Wings
I dream of wings which carry me far above human bitterness
human walls   A goose who will have no more tiny pale fluttering
goslings to bring alive   to shelter   to feed   to watch fly
off on new wings   different winds
He has a lawn this boy   A pretty face which was recently paid
thousands of dollars to be in a television commercial   I clean
their house every Wednesday morning
2 dogs which no one brushes   flying hair everywhere
A black rabbit who is almost always out of
water   usually in a filthy cage   I've cleaned the cage
out of sympathy a few times although it is not part of what
are called my duties   I check the water as soon as I arrive
This rabbit & those dogs are the boy's pets   He is very lazy
He watches television constantly leaving the sofa in the den
littered with food wrappers, soda cans, empty cereal bowls
If I'm still there when he comes home, he is rude to me   If he
has his friends with him, he makes fun of me behind my back
I muse on how he will always think of the woods
as an exciting place to kill   This family of three lives
on a five acre farm   They raise no crops   not even their own
vegetables or animals for slaughter   His father is a neurosurgeon
who longs to be a poet   His mother frantically searches
for christian enlightenment   I'm sad for her   though I don't like
her   because I know she won't find any   The boy does nothing
around the house to help without being paid   I'm 38 & still
haven't saved the amount of money he has in a passbook found
in the pillows of the couch under gum wrappers   That dead goose
This boy will probably never understand that it is not right
to take without giving   He doesn't know how to give   His mother
who cleaned & cooked the goose says she doesn't really like
to do it but can't understand why she should feel any different
about the goose than a chicken or hamburger from the supermarket

34

I bite my tongue & nod   I could explain to her that meat raised
for slaughter is very different than meat taken from the woods
where so few wild beings survive   That her ancestors are
responsible for the emptiness of this land   That lawns feed no
one   that fallow land lined with fences is sinful   That hungry
people need the food they could be growing   That spirituality
is not separate from food or wildness or respect or giving
But she already doesn't like me   because she suspects me
of reading her husband's poetry books when no one is around
& she's right   I do   I need the 32 dollars a week tolerating
them provides me   I wait for the wings on my wall to speak to me
guide my hungers   teach me winds I can't reach   I keep
these wings because walls are so hard   wildness so rare   because
ignorance must be remembered   because I am female   because I fly
only in my dreams   because I too
will have no young to let go

for Dian Million

YA DON WANNA EAT PUSSY

that Chippewa said to that gay white man who never has
Ya don wanna eat pussy after eatin hot peppers   he laughed
I stared   in the white sink memorizing rust stains
He nodded in the general direction of the windows behind us
    Two Native women chopping onions & pickles
    to make tuna fish sandwiches
    for these six men helping to move
He said   *Ya didn hear that did ya*   *Good*
She answered   *I chose to ignore it*
I muttered   *So did I*
Ya don wanna take offense at an Indian man's joke
    no matter how crude
in front of a white man
Close to my tribe   he probably guessed we're lesbians
said that   to see what we'd do
which was to keep on doin what we had been doin
That gay white man stopped talking about how much he loved
hot peppers
That Chippewa said   *Not too much for me*   *Don eat fish*
probably another joke we ignored   I said
The grocery was fresh out of buffalo & deer
Much later that gay white man called that Chippewa a drunk
    we both stared at a different floor
    in a different silence   just as sharp
    & hot

LIKE A MOTH

at twilight caught inside

searching the window for the hole back to life

to air

wings spread useless against glass

I watch the sun go down slowly over water

answers the wind could bring

are some other language

I'm caught in a web no one sees

the spider

myself

gobbling

for Cheryl Harrison

CASA COMPLETA

en este lugar donde mi hermana cree en

una religión que me exterminaría

y mi tía no deja que me acerque a sus hijos

después de que supo

y nadie se atrevió a contarle a mi abuela antes de que muriera

y aquellos como yo   se burlan de mi rareza en los bares

tú

me coses una chaqueta roja abrigada para la Navidad

me abrazas   abrazas a mi amante

le coses una chaqueta a ella también

ries con placer y exasperación ante mí

me permites

amar a tus hijos apasionadamente

Sentadas esta noche alrededor de una mesa jugando al póker

en español con tus primos

barrigas llenas de tu buena comida

en este lugar

donde he sido un tallo de dolor frío entumecido

tú me das hogar

para mi cuñada, Consuelo
Translated by Margarita Sewerin

CASA COMPLETA

in this place where my sister believes in

a religion that would murder me

& my aunt doesn't let me near her children

after she knew

& no one dared tell my grandmother before she died

& those like me   hiss at my strangeness in their bars

you

sew me a warm red jacket for Christmas

embrace me   embrace my lover

sew her a jacket too

laugh with pleasure & exasperation at me

allow me

to love your children passionately

Sitting tonight around a table playing poker

in Spanish with your cousins

bellies full of your good food

in this place

where I've been a stalk of numb cold lonely grief

you give me home

for my sister-in-law, Consuelo

SAVAGE ELOQUENCE

Big Mountain
you old story you old
thing you fighting over nothing everything
how they work us
against one another   They mean to kill us
all   Vanishing is no joke   they mean it
We don't fit this machine they've made instead of life   We breathe
spirit   softness of dirt between our toes   No metaphors
Mountains ARE our mothers   Stars our dead
Big Mountain we've heard your story a thousand times
We've grown up inside your slaughtered sheep   Move here
move there   die on the way   fences through our hearts
ask permission to gather eagle feathers   no sun dance
take our bundles   shirts   bowls to put in dry empty buildings
walls more walls jails more jails agencies thieves rapists
drunken refuge from lives with nothing left
take our children   take our hands hacked from us in death
tell lies to us   about us   lies written spoken lived
death that comes in disease relentless   Vanishing is no metaphor
Big Mountain you are no news   Our savage eloquence is dust
between their walls their thousand deaths   We go to funerals
never quite have time to step out of mourning
Everything we have left is in our hearts deeply hidden
No photograph or tape recorder or drawing can touch
the mountain of our spirits
They are Still
saying they know
what is best for us
they who know nothing
their white papers decisions empty eyes laws rules stone fences
time cut apart with dots
killing animals to hang their heads on walls
We cannot make sense of this
It has nothing   everything
to do with us
Big Mountain I've met you before in Menominee County
at Wounded Knee   on Trails of Tears
in the back street bars of every broken city

I could write a list long & thick as the books they call
Indian Law
which none of us
wrote
We know you fences death laws death hunger death
This is our skin
you take from us   These were our lives   our patterns   our dawns
the lines in our faces
which tell us our songs
Big Mountain you are too big you are too small you are such an old
old story

for Aisha Masakella

NO MORE METAPHORS

To be a prostitute is to walk cold wet streets
in a dangerous night dependent
on the hunger of strangers   vulnerable to their hatred
fists   perverse desires   diseases
To use one's face & body   literally
to pay the rent   the pimp   utilities   nylons   lipstick
to wear a bruise where the heart beats
to be a tunnel for the spit of men
to be a hole for the hatred of women
to sell one's body nightly
you could say it's
the only honest work a woman gets

To be a murderer of prostitutes
is to be free
to do it
as many times as you want
or to be warm   fed regularly
in a cell for which one pays no rent
have free tobacco   library   arts & crafts   sports programs
rehabilitation
To live to an old age
secure in tight walls
radio playing with wet dreams at night
of their bodies
breasts slashed open
their faces no longer flowers
memories of the way
it really is

for the Green River Victims

42

DOUBLE PHOENIX

She speaks burgundy birds

blue gold wings   flowers indolent on her breasts

she moves slowly her hair curled tightly

hands skimming my thighs she whispers   into my ear

I want you   my vulva shivers clenches

her mouth takes me her

tongue tells long dancing stories of flight stars darkness burst

fingers flicker in my bones

she enters me in the moment when my blood begs her

hard deep light lifts from my lips

whirls   moves tightly her mouth shivers

birds appear in my hands

my toes skim stars

I'm wings in the night sky crying out in her breasts

my hips wet flowers

for Peggy Pullen

IN THE BROTHEL CALLED AMERICA

She is on the blue path   walks against the dawn
White powder her cursed solace
Thievery & lies her language
Needle her core
No judgment in this lake of fire
She is far away as stars
Her eyes small winters of death
          Pray for her
She can't keep warm without this spoon
Takes us on a journey of defeat
Her arms black with scars
Path which comes to silence & stays
Split in the lightning of red & white
Pierced with love for women
She falls to her knees hoarsely cries
I cannot live without oblivion
          Pray for her
Let our voices lead her to another way
Pray with all our spirits
Lead her stumbling bruised ashamed
away from this dark drowning in white
          Stars give her strength
          Sun turn her eyes
          Moon guide her feet
          Earth turning hold her
          We pray for her
          We sing for her
          We drum for her
          We pray

YOUR TONGUE SPARKLES

sun on water now in my mouth memory rich as real

kisses I understand to my root   to bone ancestors where red

& so new   you speak without calluses despite our scars

Woman down my throat you stir my heart nectar where bitterness

has fought to seed

O you rainy tongue   you amaryllis tongue   you early spring

tongue   you smooth black leather tongue   you firemoon tongue

you goosebumps tongue   you soft bites tongue   you feather

tongue   you take me all in tongue   you fill me up tongue

you butter tongue   you maple syrup tongue   you rising

wind tongue   you creamy silky tongue

you fine fine tongue

you knows the way

tongue

FRESH OUT

of poetry today I polished brass all morning my feet aching as I
stood at the sink staring out the window at the hedge clipped
perfectly square by the old Filipino grandfather gardener
who no one says hello to but me   Wondering how Nina was doing
with Mrs. B. in the house next door   Mrs. is rich —always has been
crabby & stubborn, wants to go for walks at midnight   You have
to watch her & of course, her abuse   A. is worried about where
the Lesbian Resource Center will move now that the women's gym
is closing   I'm worried about Big Mountain & my younger brother
who hasn't called me in a long, long time & my other brother who
has gone back to work so soon after knee surgery because they need
the money   6 days a week planting, trimming & watering
for the rich   Our friends, the rich
Worried about whether my girlfriend & I are unraveling
Will anyone show up for the Lesbians of Color Potluck at our house
& how can I get my expensive sunglasses back from J. who doesn't
like me & thinks my calls are because I still want to sleep with her
when I gave that up years ago   only her ego prevents her from
noticing   Puget Power sent a letter saying we aren't paying
the bill on time & they want another deposit   We already know
we aren't paying on time but perhaps they have to think
of things to do   Sitting all day in an office as boring as polishing
brass   The upstairs toilet is leaking into our apartment which I
must clean before I can complain or risk eviction & when will
I have time to do that   The almighty bank is bouncing checks
I've just heard that a friend has had a fire in her place & lost much
The firemen accused her and her lover of starting the fire
I can't walk across the floor of my studio because it's piled
so high with things I have to do from a year ago   There should be
something new
which moves through me like a chinook wing of wind
Tender curling squash flowers should touch me enough to begin
but the whole garden needs weeding   I have to get the towels
from the dryer down in the laundry room   The cat has a festering
sore on his neck from a fight   Last week's dishes are still
tottering in the sink   I can't find all the poems I've already
written   There is no tower of ivory or time to build   only this
small plywood building from World War II which was meant

46

to be torn down but shows a profit if you divide up the old barracks
into apartments where the overhead tenants are all elephants
whose every cough is heard & walls mold over with damp
In winter, frequent power failures mean no heat & no way to cook
with not even enough of a belief in fame to bother sending work
out when friends request it   Tired much deeper than a few days'
rest   I could spend several years staring at nothing without
speaking then poems might begin to appear   All my friends feel
exactly the same or worse but a nut house is the only place that
will stand for silence & real bars again would kill me   The grief
I might feel at my life passing in stupid repetition of ordinary
tasks, sheds itself as I drive from job to job eating my lunch
on the way   I could tell Tillie you don't even need children
to be silent   Modern life as a poor woman can shut you up with ease
before you notice   Your typewriter can die & even the lesbian
repairwoman won't give you a break in price because the power
company wants her bill on time too & she has a child to support
by herself since the woman she had the child with   has taken off
for California with a new lover   so much for always & forever
Let's face it nowadays love is disposable & instant   You see I
could obviously rattle on this way for at least a few hours then
I could take complaints from the audience   I'm sure we could go on
for weeks if I heard all your stories   Our stories   Who will
remember them for us? Who will take care of us when we're old?
Poetry mashed out of our bodies withering preparing to go back to
earth & stars   We'll know then   how we've squandered our lives
living for cheap thrills   a new woman   & a better VCR
Listen Sun   you girl that gets up every morning before the rest
of us & hauls ass across the whole damn sky every day all day until
your feet hurt too
Listen Sun   give me
a little courage
for this joint

for Sky Yarbrough

ESTA NOCHE SOÑÉ OTRA VEZ CON ESA PLAYA

en El Salvador donde la policía secreta tira a aquellos
con los que ha terminado
Fotografía que me persigue   jadeante no me deja quieta
Esqueletos mezclados con partes de cuerpos caras y manos hinchadas
por torturas grotescas   Los familiares de esta gente indígena
vienen aquí   para buscar a sus desaparacidos
madres, padres, hermanas, hermanos, amantes, amigas, amigos
para llevarse huesos o carne podrida sus manos cortadas con dolor
Me despierto gritando   *Qué es esta enfermedad*   Qué es este
odio que va más allá del aliento de mi corazón
Esta enfermedad que mata a la piel morena una y otra y otra vez
a través del mundo   Ahora
en estos momentos mientras nos estamos
mirando conteniendo lágrimas que no salvan a nadie
Racismo una palabra demasiado chica
Los números de desaparecidos son más
que los granos de arena donde ellos yacen
Mis manos son huesos de pena por mis familiares
que se encuentran tan lejos   cuyo lenguaje yo no hablo
cuya sopa yo no compartiré   cuyas vidas son la mía reflejada
Nuestra impotencia frente a la policía secreta   picanas eléctricas
puños   cuchillos   cadenas   me tortura constantemente
Mi voz no puede remediarlo
Mi corazón no puede soportarlo
Mi vida se desgarra con memorias antiguas   Los mismos genitales
blandidos en las espadas de caballerías hace cien años en esta tierra
ahora se pudren en El Salvador   El tiempo mueve un entretejido
continuo de aniquilación
De qué sirve una poetisa contra la policía secreta
        Nuestra carne frágil tierna
De qué sirve una poetisa contra el hambre
        Nuestras barrigas hambrientas   .
De qué sirve una poetisa contra el dolor desgarrado por temor
                                        desgarrado por odio

I DREAMT AGAIN TONIGHT OF THAT BEACH

in El Salvador where the secret police dump
those they are finished with
Photograph that comes after me panting   won't leave me alone
Skeletons mixed with partial bodies   faces & hands bloated
with grotesque tortures   The relatives of these Native people
come here   to search for their missing
mothers, fathers, sisters, brothers, lovers, friends
to carry away bones or rotting flesh their hands cut with grief
I wake up shrieking   *What is this disease*   What is it this
hatred beyond my heart's breath   This disease which kills
brown skin over & over & over   throughout the world   Now
in this moment as we look at one another
holding in tears that save no one
Racism too small a word   The numbers of disappeared are more
than the grains of sand on which they lay
My hands are bones of grief for my relatives so far away
whose language I don't speak   whose soup I won't share
whose lives are my own reflected
Our helplessness in the face of secret police   electric probes
fists   knives   chains   tortures me constantly
My voice cannot heal this
My heart cannot bear this
My life tears open with ancient memories   The same genitals
brandished on cavalry swords one hundred years ago in this land
rot now in El Salvador   Time moves a continuous weave
of annihilation
What good is a poet against secret police
     Our tender fragile flesh
What good is a poet against starvation
     Our hungering bellies
What good is a poet against grief torn by fear torn by hatred

Nuestra sangre se acelera con memorias
Esa enfermedad
El sudor de mis sueños me despierta   Yo sé que si hubiera nacido
en El Salvador
tu estarías buscándome esta noche en
Esa Playa

Translated by Juanita Ramos
assisted by Margarita Sewerin

Our blood rushing with memories
That disease
My dreams sweat me awake   I know that if I had been born
in El Salvador
you would be looking for me tonight on
That Beach

GALLOPING

through gold our hooves

spin autumn stars

wide eyes flicker   scarlet   sepia   lemon

cedar   madronna   fir

alder   birch   pine

staghorn sumac

manes flow   smoky lace fingers

tails dance a pink sky

long our legs

are fire

for Jackie Davenport

COMING HOME
February 21, 1972 —March 1, 1987

from a long week
of convincing young white college women that
racism is real
She meets me at the airport with a face gray as rain
What is it?   *Is one of the cats dead?*   No
I make jokes   Assume her strangeness is the fight we had
before I left   We collect my bags
Thousands of strangers rush past us   mostly white
Once in the car safe behind tinted windows she says
as gently as possible
Rahkisha's dead   Sunday around nine
her heart stopped   Rain down my face
The streets rain puddles & accidents   I notice forsythia
blooming along the freeway   think of Forsythe County
in Georgia where in 1987 South Africa is alive in America
a county for whites only
She was fifteen   A young Black woman who preferred
the Beastie Boys to thinking of Georgia
Later   at the memorial service   spring flowers
too many huge urns of forsythia   & a white ribbon
printed in gold across my roses   saying
We'll miss you Kisha
Her teenage friends weep open as sky while the older ones sit stiff
& unblooming   Some of us hear the Beastie Boys for the first time
In the front with the teenagers where her sister sat me
wearing new silver sneakers with stars on the ankles
that I knew Kisha would have loved & borrowed
my grief is not safe   not free

STRIPPING LUNARIA

tiny brown fans scatter on the floor despite my care
    I imagine each seed   a plume of magenta blossoms
    planted near the Scotch broom in the field beside us
This is peasant labor   done by hand   these moony
stalks will stay with me   Next year   I'll sell my crop
    You want me to be completely honest
as though after these years in an opaque white world
    pods stripped of seed
in this sterile aftermath I could point to a piece of debris
    & claim it true
Washed up here I'm opened like plumes around the moon
    turning away I stalk any story that will let me see
    another spring   Silvery paper thin   I could be honest
stripped of lessons learned deep in seeds of sticks
    at my head legs back   fists in the face   missing teeth
    Lost years   Lost home   dirty bread pissed on
that white boys forced me to eat   cornered at seven
my heart beating with terror I knew how much more they could do
    how little anyone would care
chased   learned to lie   to smile when afraid
    to be silent instead of cry
I've scattered myself common loose as wildflower seed
Peeling these layers each edge is brown uneven different
to be completely honest I would first need to be full as a moon
    journey I'm on as I gather myself off the floor
    where I fall each time a look strips me
The seed sprouts   My heart has frosts that kill
Let's see if I can bloom next summer   make seeds for another spring
    then we'll speak of
        honesty

for BJ

Gift: & Blue Heron   Chrystos 1988

FOR ELI

I

Usually I don't read newspapers/can't/awhile ago someone
left you in my car or
your face was precise gray dots where I sat to eat
Are you here Eli   Come
sit in my lap/let me rock you/explain with some meaningless words
that your daddy didn't mean
to beat you to death
although we both know
he probably did
We're strangers/you're safer with me
I hear your tape-recorded cries as I sleep restless
my head unshed tears/I shout at strangers
to speak up
It's all that's left of you/faint gray dots/police evidence
a mother hollowed
why didn't she
help you
they all want to know/she was hiding out under
the Father Knows Best rock with the rest of us
she's a woman/even the American Psychiatric Association has charts
to prove   she's not   a person   an adult
she's your big sister like me ducking blows that you're too small
to escape
You've escaped now/they want to talk about the tragedy
what do they know of survival/nightmares/chronic mistrust/
erupting paranoia/being locked up until you become the animal
they say you are
of the moment when backed into your own grief/terror/despair
you could beat your son as you were beaten/are beaten
There's no excuse
What will we do with your poppa now that you walk with stars
Beat him to death
Fry him to death
Talk him to death
They say/even his cellmates at the prison wanted nothing
to do with him
Is that because he is Cherokee

56

How lonely/is a man/who beats his son to death
One half himself
Tortured you/pencils up your ass
I've had/things/stuck up/me too/by those who were
taking care of me
Maybe that's why I get odd chills/at the words uttered casually
Take Care/as though I have a choice in the matter
Rage still   some unseen beast/erupts anytime/to gnaw my heart
Eli   could I smooth the hair from your forehead
Abstract tenderness possible/because you never/woke me up at 3 a.m.
on a work night/screaming with an earache/until I was ready to kill
for silence
Eli you are not unusual/you simply got press
coverage/briefly/knocked aside quickly enough
by failed disarmament talks
We couldn't disarm your daddy either
his rage/his lost compassion/his shriveled kicked-in soul
Eli go to sleep now

II

They ask me if I'll have children
a question repeated so often I'm forced
to answer   *No*
I raised my brothers & sister while my mother was too depressed
to go on/my father gone   *No*
Give a child this world full of the deaths of children?
Bring a girl child to one chance in three of being raped?
To the barbarous fact of torture here & there?
Bring new life to this dump we've made in greed & stupidity?
Bring a child to hear me complain about the overdue rent/price
of cauliflower/endless fight for a moment of peace/silence/grace
To the certainty   of my angry hands lashing
Bring you here again Eli   No
I could not do that

III

At the laundromat a woman I know slightly begins to talk
about a book she is reading on creativity
the author believes all writing/painting/dancing is motivated
by fear
Immediately I think of you Eli
Am I most afraid of your father who lost his soul/before you
were born/or your mother who denied the evidence of her eyes
bruises/broken teeth/marks across your back
when she was bathing you Eli   What was in her mind
Did she give up her soul/to love your father
Am I most afraid of this rage in myself/reflected like a splinter
buried deep in the palm
Your father could be/myself
backed far enough into walls that won't give
He's crazy/pleads not guilty to the murder charge/that's what
the lawyers probably told him to do
We'd rather die/than go back to jail
Eli you've already forgotten him/Safe now
back in the stars walking/they say/with God
As we fold our clothes in neat sane piles
I tell her I'm writing about you/her face closes
as so often happens to me/I'm too intense/speak
the unspeakable
She veers into the subject of her son who is involved
with a woman who just had a baby/not his
Not long ago/she read of an 18 year old boy/charged
with murdering his girlfriend's son
She's afraid   *That's not my baby*
she says   *He lives with his father now/I hadn't seen him in two*
years/This February he was a stranger to me   Not
my baby now   & her arms
unconsciously form a cradle in front of her breast
Her eyes blank with unspoken panic
Eli she would have protected you I think   as I would have
Easy now to surmise/to offer you shelter   Eli
will you ever/forgive us/for allowing one troubled man
too much power

58

Who   will comfort your mother
with her photograph ghosts/Who can swallow their disgust enough
to heal her
Can she be healed
Daily I expect news that she's hung herself or been confined
to a mental prison/Perhaps like Charles Manson's women/she's too
far away for anything/as easy as that
This lesson repeats itself/We're capable of anything
Each of us/Chance pushes us toward torture/We women trained
from birth to be decorative/to be amiable/to nurture
participate/when we don't stop it
Suddenly/I see myself/part of a circle/children watching
as Alan W./white bully of our block/pulled down the pants
of a small boy named Bruce with a retarded sister/humiliated him
beat his bare butt with a stick
I thought I was too small to stop him/Sick to my stomach
told no one/None of us did/not even Bruce
Somewhere today Alan W. is probably a successful businessman
he had that kind of heart/I wonder if he tortures his children
or perhaps prostitutes on his lunch hour
Where is he/so I can vomit on him
Eli your mother/is more mystery to me than your father
It's so easy to be simple-minded/We accept whatever it is
that is said to us
We're the helpless women
helping anyway

IV

Eli I once lived with a little boy who was the son of my lover
I'm deeply ashamed to say/I could not love him
I sent them away/when I knew
She begins to forgive me now/but he   Eli
he won't look at me/I don't exist/he's killed me
to survive my not loving him
I understand so well that I don't try to push past his rage
Everyone/says/he was so much better behaved/after he lived with me
Yes/but I was exhausted/angry with our battle of wills
He was accustomed to anarchy/to running the show/to kicking
everyone   to taking whatever he wanted/to refusing meals out of
whim   & I   Eli/I was so often/very hungry/as a child

I couldn't be the one to break
him/make him
a reasonable person to live with   I wanted
privacy/time to write/silence
His aggression/exuberance frightened me/Eli   I can hardly
say this/failure of spirit/& you/Jamie Lee/can't hear me now/
as I scrape out the words sour in my mouth
I'm so sorry/it was for your own good
It is
Some people simply shouldn't have children/I'm one of them
Eli   your father is another

V

My father/the unwanted residue of a marriage between red & white
that both worlds opposed/His mother died when he was nine/
His father locked up in a mental prison/Beaten from one place
to another/not old enough to be useful/until he ran away
to be a hobo at 13
My mother/neglected disliked second daughter of a woman
who craved only sons/seethes with hatred/she can't admit/as a good
Catholic girl   They hit me/I survived/thrown against walls/
sticks that broke/coat hangers/yardsticks/belts/fists
I was older when violence converged/five by then/my father gone
most of the time/which is probably why I'm alive
& you Eli are dead
Beaten for crying when I was beaten I learned to be
silent
to sexual abuse/gang rape/beatings from lovers/from strangers
Eli if you had lived I could not promise you better
Beaten too often/one has ruts where it is so easy
to be beaten again
It is all I can do/to love those who won't beat me/because they
are such strangers
Eli I want you to be the last child who dies/I want your death
to have meaning
I'm so glad
you're not alive
to know that it doesn't

VI
I asked her if this was good enough
Good enough for what?   To stop it
No/only when you get rid of all the men/will it stop
But you Eli were a man & it's not as easy as that
There have been a few isolated women
who have tortured/killed children
The disease not gender or race or class specific
Those who beat children are under heels twisting them
ground down to pulp in factories/prisons/K Marts/welfare
Perhaps money helps/one hires a nanny to change the diapers/calm
the midnight terrors   But it isn't the caretaking that causes fury
It's no job/garbage in the halls/elephant neighbors overhead/
eviction notices/overdue bills/outrageous "security" deposits
from landlords & power companies/No one gives a damn about you
why don't you just pack up/get lost
your misery is all your own fault   So easy
so easy to be polite/when you've got enough money to grease
your feet down the rails
Rich women/I've known/carry bitterness in their bags/because
they feel/their mothers didn't care about them/paid others to
Perhaps we could figure out/how to raise children
if we can get to the moon

VII
Most of the children I know/think I'm wonderful/I can be
for two or three hours/listen instead of endure/make magic
jokes/drawings/secrets   If they were my own
I would not be able to endure/selfish/dreamy/a child now myself
I don't want to pay/that much attention/often can't afford
to feed myself
Eli I could be you/your father/your mother
I could be the waitress who noticed you only able to eat ice cream
because your mouth was bloody pulp/She wanted to take you home
Looking for a last time at your smiling face gray/smudged
I lose faith   my edges curl
Eli I cry/in my heart/for you/with a dry face
I'm so afraid
in a world where your daddy could beat you/to death
plead
not guilty

OUT THE TOP I GO

leave my body like an autumn leaf

head straight for the rolling

cloud people   Sing   Laugh   juicy with it

whirl round til I'm dizzy

hot with sky bread   Jump from blue to yellow to night

go see the moon   Stick some stars in my teeth & hair

race a thunderbolt lightning streak

Grow a horse to gallop through the sunrise flying

into some birds with a feast to share

Go out the bottom of the bowl

cruising down to black holes in a racy convertible

hair slicked back   looking for

trouble & something to drink

Turn into a buffalo munching on prairie sky

tell the sun a joke   she laugh so hard she fall over

unexpected darkness   Just a volcano

Hard

to come back here

after all that fooling around

for Elizabeth Woody

BITTER TEETH

about my uncle, Jean LeMaitré

Rummaging in these old shoes   rain clouds   frost stars
worn out socks   snarls of hair   broken needs   dead leaves
I heave you to any black hole   No space deep enough or far
    Every word we spoke   Each kiss taken   Years your cock
down my throat   hissing nightmares   Shape you pressed in me
    concubine   lying   cheating   warped commodity   no future
looking at too many ceilings   not enough air   I ache
    for your funeral   Only place safe to see you again
I'll spit in your face for once
    So young I
So long your tongue taught me tricks   I sweep my porch look to sky
    You're 750 miles away & don't have my address
You're behind my back
    Praying for relief I've buried you therapied you
talked you into blue streaks & scars   cut my arms   my breasts
    expelled a thousand seeds   Wet clay to your fist I
couldn't drink enough   shoot up enough   spread my legs enough
    hundreds of strangers & worse
        to wipe you out
I'm afraid as I die I'll still want to bite out your heart chew
    to feel the gush
        Scrape it clean
            new infection erupts
                scrape scrape
                rhymes with your word

BAG LADY
a monologue from the play, *Rudey Toot Zoo*

They call Indians & Negroes a thief. Now one of these people they stole from their own country & the other one they stole their own country from. Now you tell me who is the thief? WHO is the thief? & lazy! HA! I never seen nothing lazier than a white man. Even built a machine to sharpen knives. Ridiculous. Some spit & a stone is all you need. Listen, I've cleaned white houses since I was 15 & I'll tell you nobody is lazier. They'll vomit in a sink & not even bother to rinse it down. Wait for the cleaning woman to come. I spit at them. Yes I do. Sit everyday on Fifth & Pine & I spit at them going by. They ACT like I'm not there but you'll notice they stay out of my range.

No, no, I never been in that love stuff. I watched my mother & 3 older sisters cry & cry over men. No siree, I'm free & never cried for no one. Never let a man beat me or cut me or rape me or cuss me. I learned young to be mean enough to be safe. Don't even bother to think you can touch me. People are walking bags of disease. Less you deal with them, the happier you'll be. No that love stuff will tear your ass up. Don't ever be fool enough to think because you got somebody in your pants today means you won't be lonely tomorrow. No honey, lonely is what we all come to. You can't do nothing to change it so you might as well get used to it. All that crap they feed you about meeting your soulmate. We're all hacked willy nilly out of clay falling this way & that. Nobody matches. You want to pretend you do, you gotta fold up whole parts of yourself & let em die. No no. Human betrayals know no bounds. I'd rather be born a panther but I'm stuck here. No panthers left anyhow except their heads stuck up on some damn white man's walls. Glass eyes. Most people got glass eyes. They don't see nothing but themselves. Not even themselves. You think your electric toaster & hair dryer & stove & car are gonna protect you from your death. No they won't. I live today like I'm gonna die tomorrow. Don't pretend to own nothing. Cause when you're dead you're just some cold smelly meat. No matter how many toasters you think you own.

No, honey I'm not happy. Nobody's happy. Happy is just an advertising gimmick. You buy their thing & then you're "happy." Or you do what they want you to do & then you're "happy." Oh that happy shit is the biggest con game going. People pretending to be happy a mile a minute. Darlin I'm ALIVE & that's all you need. I laugh a lot more than some happy folks.

I don't belong here. Not anywhere. Used to think I was from outer space & my people was long overdue to pick me up & take me home. Now I think I just told myself that to make it hurt less to be here. Oh I'll tell you this world has more pain than anybody can stand.

So people watch TV. Go bowling. Write stories. Glue macaroni on cardboard & spray it gold. Everything everybody be doing so intently all the time is just ways to get away from that pain.

Pretend we got control. The universe could get sick of us tonight & blow us to bits with a meteor.

Pain & fear. That's what this whole world run on. I look em both in the eye every morning when I get out of my dumpster. Now you go on now my feet hurt & I don't want to talk to you no more.

especially for Karen Timentwa

I AM NOT YOUR PRINCESS

Sandpaper between two cultures which tear
one another apart I'm not
a means by which you can reach spiritual understanding or even
learn to do beadwork
I'm only willing to tell you how to make fry bread
1 cup flour, spoon of salt, spoon of baking powder
Stir   Add milk or water or beer until it holds together
Slap each piece into rounds   Let rest
Fry in hot grease until golden
This is Indian food
only if you know that Indian is a government word
which has nothing to do with our names for ourselves
I won't chant for you
I admit no spirituality to you
I will not sweat with you or ease your guilt with fine turtle tales
I will not wear dancing clothes to read poetry or
explain hardly anything at all
I don't think your attempts to understand us are going to work so
I'd rather you left us in whatever peace we can still
scramble up   after all you continue to do
If you send me one more damn flyer about how to heal myself
for $300 with special feminist counseling
I'll probably set fire to something
If you tell me one more time that I'm wise I'll throw up on you
Look at me
See my confusion   loneliness   fear   worrying about all our
struggles to keep   what little is left for us
Look at my heart   not your fantasies   Please don't ever
again tell me about your Cherokee great-great grandmother
Don't assume I know every other Native Activist
in the world personally   That I even know names of all the tribes
or can pronounce names I've never heard
or that I'm expert at the peyote stitch

If   you ever
again tell me
how strong I am
I'll lay down on the ground & moan so you'll see
at last   my human weakness   like your own
I'm not strong   I'm scraped
I'm blessed with life while so many I've known are dead
I have work to do   dishes to wash   a house to clean
There is no magic
See my simple cracked hands which have washed the same things
you wash   See my eyes dark with fear in a house by myself
late at night   See that to pity me or to adore me
are the same
1 cup flour, spoon of salt, spoon of baking powder, liquid to hold
Remember this is only my recipe   There are many others
Let me rest
here
at least

especially for Dee Johnson

ELEGY FOR HILLS

Father gone again Mother locked in room Bathrobe all day
Or screaming Stick & broom tattoo Throw school books at us
Why can't you kids   Boiling fury Poor abandoned mother
Bills at her throat Lonely Frightened What If
Can't grab coat Just get away Out Her screaming
You goddamn whore walking the streets again   I'm ten
silent because beaten if I answer Out Relief Quickly to the last
few hills city hasn't swallowed   Deeper relief

Soft   you could roll down through prickers laughing   find
a cardboard box   wax it with a candlestick &
WWWHHHHOOOOOOOOoooo! to the bottom roaring with speed
& the long line where sky touches
earth   Golden except in spring   Dry
coming together at the bottom in cleavage so deep
    you could stick your foot down & not touch ANYTHING
Olive trees sprawled   drunken robins flew like eagles
Blue belly lizards   when the poppies & lupine bloomed you could
hardly not burst from the beauty   The old Japanese man's
rows of prized iris that he sold downtown   Chased us
with his rifle when we went running through his tender
shoots   Last farmer surrounded by factories hanging
on with his tongue   We rode his cow   She knelt down
pitched us over her head into cowpies   laughing
I didn't know until years later that we were souring her milk
& I understood the rifle
    A color no where else
    Gentle maybe tan maybe silver maybe gold
breathing hard running jackrabbit my heart pattering drum
old olive tree great grandma safe at last scramble into rough
bark skinning knees & hide   pounding blue sky haze of factories
choking in   those hills hanging on with their last grass
    Golden   warm   open   Bugs & dirt   prickers to throw at one
another   Riding down   running over   they were
my mother & father   Cried there   thought   buried dead animals
    watched   began to be   evening pink hazy dusk you could see
stars   before the lights blotted them out   a silence there

I've carried with me through streets   hassles   fights
knives in alleys   tricks   fists   gun at sister's head   thieves
rapists   deaths   bars   bruises   drugs & beer
In two years
golden
became gray #3742, gray #3744, white #3746, charcoal #3748
dingy #3750, dead #3752
thousands more
They call it civilization

especially for Dian Million

BONES

I was born on the streets of a war-swollen city my Daddy
bringing home whores & bums to sleep on the couch
   of my Mother's appalled virgin tight stove apartment
   because they had nowhere else to go
forty years later she's still angry with him
   I've brought home many a whore & bum in his honor
been a whore & bum myself with nowhere else to go
     O Daddy maybe we'll talk some day
maybe I'll lay you down in your grave without a moment to spare
   a moment to know   to lose   to touch
Daddy they send for me at Yale   want me to show them power
   I do   while I'm looking for the back door way out fire escape
   I get paid
Daddy I was supposed to go to college because you didn't
   worked & fled all your life so I could have more
   you're sad to see
I seem to have chosen less
less only in the shiny mirror gadget geegaws twisted greed place
   where things eat up things
Daddy you can take me to Yale   but they don't ask me back
   I've got you in my belly as well as myself
   I'm an arrow you want to ride   makes me too strong
   they stick with fear   cut me   *O Daddy*
     can't even send this

I HAVE NOT SIGNED A TREATY
WITH THE U.S. GOVERNMENT

nor has my father nor his father
nor any grandmothers
We don't recognize these names on old sorry paper
Therefore we declare the United States a crazy person
       nightmare   lousy food   ugly clothes   bad meat
       nobody we know
No one wants to go there   This U.S. is theory   illusion
terrible ceremony   The United States can't dance   can't cook
       has no children   no elders   no relatives
They build funny houses no one lives in but papers
       Everything the United States does to everybody is bad
No this U.S. is not a good idea   We declare you terminated
       You've had your fun now go home we're tired   We signed
no treaty   WHAT are you still doing here   Go somewhere else &
       build a McDonald's   We're going to tear all this ugly mess
down now   We revoke your immigration papers
       your assimilation soap suds   your stories are no good
your colors hurt our feet   our eyes are sore
       our bellies are tied in sour knots   Go Away Now
       We don't know you from anybody
You must be some ghost in the wrong place   wrong time
       Pack up your toys   garbage   lies
We   who are alive now
       have signed no treaties
Burn down your stuck houses   your sitting
       in a nowhere gray gloom   Your spell is dead
Go so far away we won't remember you ever came here
       Take these words back with you

especially for Celeste George

DEAR MR. PRESIDENT

I am a woman with 3 children   a husband who has been out of work
for 18 months & no place to go
I am one of 400 families
Emergency Housing has turned away this month
The 399 others are no consolation to me
This is an emergency
Mr. P. I am a mother of two who lives with my mother
who can no longer work
Someone reported to welfare that I was working
My checks have been temporarily stopped pending investigation
I think my ex-boyfriend's mother called them for spite
because I don't have a job
although I have submitted over 200 resumes in the last year & a half
We got evicted   Emergency Housing can't find us anything
This is an Emergency
Hey Mr. Prez   My boyfriend was beating me & the kids so bad
I just had to get out before one of us was killed
The battered women's is full & so is emergency housing
The worker said she'd already turned away 378 this month
We're living in my car & cooking at my mother's studio apartment
in the old people's housing   This is an emergency
400 times a month in one city that bothers to try & fix it
times 2 years
is a class of people
It is worse in other towns
When we have no place to live
Dear Mr. Pay Attention now
we are not in economic recovery
We are   an emergency

for Damita Jo Brown

72

TABLE MANNERS

I sit down with my plate to eat
    You're Indian aren't you?
    Yes
    What tribe are you?
    Menominee
    What?
    Menominee
    What?
    Me   Nom   I   Nee
    Is that your name or your tribe?
    My tribe, Great Lakes region
    What?
    Great Lakes region
    So you're from Wisconsin
    No, I was born in San Francisco
    Oh well what are you doing here I mean
    that's pretty far   Do you still live there?
    No, I live in Seattle
    Oh, that's pretty far north
    Yes
    What group are you in?
    The residents who are here to write instead of take classes
    What?   Oh   So when did you start writing?
    When I was nine
    Oh well then   I guess you'd better keep up with it
    Yes
During this entire conversation   my fist clenched at my place
polite mask tied firmly to my head with barbed wire
I sat   until I could get up casually
plate in hand
seem to move away without intent
to a bench with no one else
so as not to insult her
who had ruined my meal

for Denise Tuggle, who has had to sit with a few of these too

WHITE GIRL DON'T

tell me about El Salvador or Nicaragua
especially if you go there for an educational
vacation
Tell me about First Street in Seattle
the bench where the drunk Indians hang out
tell me how long we've been wearing these same clothes
& when was the last time
we had something good
to eat
Tell me about the uranium pilings we've built our houses
out of down in Four Corners
Tell me about seeing your supposed people endlessly flickering
across gray screens & still
being called savages
White girl don't
tell me about South Africa
Tell me about the streets of Philadelphia
where a Black man slept in the snow & nobody cared but me
Tell me about being an eleven year old girl
whose leg is shot off
because she was accidentally in the way of an argument
the numbers runner is having with the Mafia Man
Tell me about having a mother so drunk
she can't take care of you because she knows
even sober she couldn't give you what you need
For every hungry belly you want to blame
on somebody else somewhere else
exotic or romantic
I can show you ten bellies here
empty as your words
Don't talk to me
about the prison conditions in Russia or Peru or Argentina
Let me take you to Purdy white girl
I'll show you some torture that works & works & works
doesn't leave a mark
Somewhere else is safer & not your fault & not your responsibility

Easy
to be outraged & run off to save somebody
on your white horse airplane
come back with slides to show me how horrible it is down there
gore gleaming in your eyes   your excitement just
held in
I'll show you blood on every street in america
We aren't the latest fad in your candy-striper life
You want genocide
look out the window at the road going past your house
honey
it's killing us
Don't send me letters asking me to mail you money
so you can go here or there
to see how things are
You need an eye exam right here in this town
I've got El Salvador & South Africa in my throat
when I stare down two white ladies
staring at me in the fish & chips
When I go on vacation
if I ever have the gall to ask you to send me money
I'm going to stay right here
just not clean toilets for two weeks
which will be quite   educational
stop crying   stop whining
Don't aim 5,000 miles away to a land whose words
you barely speak   if at all
Right here now   genocide
I'll tell you about it

for Jackie Moorey

CROONING

A soft old song for every lesbian who wants
                    to go home
                         again & can't
with her woman lover in her arms
    holding hands in the streets   simple in our love
that they twist so   No lies   Not "cousins"
    not "best friends"   not "roommates"
No second bedrooms for show   no pretend boyfriends
    no custody cases   no hidden mouths   no grim smiles
at queer jokes on the job you'd lose
    if they knew
Go Home   with joy & strength
    go home   be received instead of tolerated
No anguished mothers afraid of father's response or
    neighbors' gossip or grandma's heart condition
        Go home to a clean welcome mat
                    a double bed
no questions   accusations   or expectations
    I croon an old soft song for us
rocking down to a kind place we won't see in our lives
                    fighting for it
even when we're drunk in bars
                    because we
                    can't go home
                         Crooning for us   my heart split

for Ana R. Kissed

I WAS OVER ON THE REZ

one hot hot Saturday blue sky   Everybody except me   was
drinking beer & moving slow   Cassie was inside watching an old
Avengers re-run   She really loves that Emma Peel   Ron was
listening to reggae on the headphones   Lisa was outside on a lounge
chair borrowed from the neighbors   resting her back which had
been bad for weeks   Don't know where Gary was   I watched the
Avengers for awhile & got restless   Decided to go down to the
beach with the dogs & throw the tennis ball   So we strolled down
the road listening to the birds   going slowly because Beaumont has
a bum leg from where a car hit him   He whimpers as he goes   Not
even a tiny wind blew the leaves   All the shadows still   I wanted
to be alone to write but unless you walk for three miles inland that
part of the Rez is very noisy & congested   It's the town where most
of the whites live with 2 bars on main street which doesn't have a
name   They were formerly known as the Indian bar & the white bar
but are now "integrated" with disastrous results   There's a thrift
store which changes names & owners about every 6 months but
continues to sell the same dreary stuff that nobody wants   Across
the street is the Tribal Police with petunias growing in a box   a
grocery store which sells green meat & the all-volunteer fire
department which has the only free ambulance service in the state
which is a point of loud pride   The white people live overlooking
the water in houses much too big for their lots & close enough so you
hear your neighbors' toilets flush   For the most part everyone gets
along   which means the whites hang out together & buy fireworks
in July from the Rez stands & the Indians hang out somewhere else
most of the time   Occasionally there are bloody fights in one of the
bars   After the last one   BJ gave mouth to mouth resuscitation to
an Indian guy from out by Little Boston who got his ribs under some
trucker's cowboy boots   She's   the only reason he lived   They
had to call the ambulance   Everybody went away shaking their
heads saying   *LOOK at those boots!   Those BOOTS man!*
You could say that there is less tension here than on some other
reservations where I've been   Probably because it never stays too
hot for too long   Unemployment isn't too bad because of the Navy
base nearby & this is where the tribe was in the first place   They also

throw a big Pow Wow in the summer that whites love to come to
And the main thing is there is no oil   gold   uranium
diamonds or silver in the dirt as far as we know   We'll be the first to
go in a nuclear war because of the base   which is fine by me
People are already so mean I wouldn't want to survive & see how
they'd get with no TV
So walking down past the bar through the gravel around the Tribal
Youth Center which is a little house with peeling white paint   we
headed to the beach   Some white guys in a big Winnebago towing
a boat started making lewd disgusting comments at me   Which is
why I took the dogs   Gives me a perfect excuse to shout *BAD DOG*
make an ugly face at the ground & go on without acknowledging
those men at all   The dogs understand perfectly who the real trouble
is   Near the water there were some hippies drinking beer so we
went the other way   There was old Charley heaped against the
driftwood pretty drunk   He called to me to drink with him & I said
Hi   shook my head & kept going   The dogs got happily wet &
didn't cut their paws on any of the broken glass all over the rocks   I
collected as much of it as I could carry to take back to the recycling bin
up on the highway   I felt a cold place in my breast & glanced down
A blond boy was grabbing old Charley's hat & slapping him with it
playfully   He took Charley's glasses & put them on the hat brim
Grabbed his empty bottle & broke it against the stones of the cliff
So I went down to see if Charley was going to be ok   His face has
the wrinkles of someone who's survived many beatings   As I came
up on them   the kid slowed a little & looked at me   His eyes
weren't full of the hate I expected   I said   *Maybe you should find
somebody else to play with*   His blank eyes told me that nobody his
own age would play with him & it looked like his family wasn't too
interested either   *Why*   he says   *he's my friend*   Charley was in
a state not to care about cruelty or pride or much of anything   So I
shrugged   Charley stared straight into my eyes & told the dog to
bite me   I knew why   I wasn't drunk   I was angry with Charley
for letting the kid treat him like that   I was ashamed   because he is
old & I need to respect him   Because it was none of my business &
all of it   I had no right to say a thing   Or think it   I'm not
willing to take Charley home & care for him   Because it was too hot
to think or feel & I was a reminder that he could if

I stared back as though I was a hot drunk sky until he reached to shake
my hand   our truce formed   He wanted me to go buy him a bottle
with his crumpled dollar   I couldn't   If he could have moved
he too would have shrugged   I walked up the dry grass pitching
rocks hard into the dirt mumbling about white kids under my breath
to the dogs   But really   it was Charley who hurt   He could have
been my dead Grandpa who died locked up in a county home   He
could be making beautiful cedar canoes   He could have a garden of
beans & potatoes coming ripe now   Instead he's the stereotype I've
fought all my life often as cruelly judgmental as any white person
I've written this sitting on the porch with everyone talking around
me   BJ playing the guitar blues   The cat twitching her tail on my
toe   Everyone's hungry & waiting on me to finish up & go over to
Poulsbo to get a pizza   I'm the only one sober enough to drive
Now BJ is brushing my hair   I could cry if I didn't have to explain
It's not anything   Just can't get Charley out of my throat   Maybe I
should get the dog to bite me   Not hard   Just enough to place the
pain   BJ just bit me as she read over my shoulder & we laugh with a
tinny taste of tears under our tongues

especially for Viv Haskell

Gift: Eagle   Chrystos 1988

FOR CRYSTAL REBECCA

Sunday night we're sitting around the table greasy
with rice   BBQ ribs & scattered peas
    because your baby brother Manley is still learning spoons
You're on my lap
earnestly copying words I've printed for you
from the bottom up
    Your delight & surprise at each
    W or *O* finished   colors my heart
Leaning back in my arms your eyes are dark with happiness
    I'm your Tia   with no children of my own
Your fingers trace my name on my shirt
which you copy   admiring the diamonds
You shake your head seriously
when I tell you they're only rhinestones
You insist clearly that they're diamonds   & they become so
We laugh so hard at Manley throwing the rice into the salad
    Shyly   you say to me in a whisper
            Manley will get OLD like me
I remember when 5   was very old
My fingers are orange from your Crayola marker
        I don't want to wash
I save the poem you made of the words I wrote for you
very seriously   framing it in oak   for my kitchen
    where it shines saying
            Chrystos
            like Rebecca
            laughs birds
            the colors I love you
& oh how I do

81

TOLSTOY

the great writer
         who cared so much for the poor
             they say
seduced
a virgin serving girl in his aunt's house
She was dismissed
Later he wrote a novel   His wife wrote in her diary
that he described   . . . *fornication between the serving girl*
& the officer with the peculiar
relish of a gastronome
eating something tasty
His wife   ought to know
    The serving girl probably had his child
probably died young
certainly the child died without ever learning to read or write
     or meeting his father
ALL   we know of her
is her name   Masha

for Uta Fellechner

82

MY GRANDMOTHER LOOKS OUT OF MY EYES

Two white boys   11 or 12   with high voices
jeer
at a third who follows with head down
Hey he's got shit on his toes!
Yeah fart face!
One pisses against the crumbling garage wall
tosses his head & leers when he sees I've seen him
He's the one with an air gun he brandishes as he hoots
They shut up the birds & wind with their racket
Yeah hey look at him stupid ass!   Yeah you eat your own shit!
Yeah hurry up manglefoot!   Their lips are dog snarls
I watch them closely up the road
Shouting & braying there they go
        in cavalry blue & gray

for Mary McGough

SHE IS TOO FRIGHTENED

to write this herself   would not want me to use her name
as shaking she tries to stand being around my family or anybody
At ease only when completely alone in the woods   Otherwise drugs
or drinking or any old thing to endure america
Hungry & small her body is tight with scars where her adopted
mother beat her   Threw her out the window   where nightmares
come every night   I've learned before she's awake to say
It's ok   It's ok   & she goes back to those tunnels
where her life has twisted her dry   Longing to be held
she reaches for me when I have no more to give but do
because she only trusts 2 people & I am one of them
Choking on the suicide of her brother & secrets too large
to eat for breakfast   Bashing her head in accidentally
as I do when scared   Taking drugs the system says will give
her relief & they don't   Desperate enough to kill a stranger
nothing helps   Sometimes we can get her to laugh
by pretending to be the Three Stooges or Donald Duck or
sarcastically making fun of white folks
We happened to meet her on a street corner & it's a good
thing/as she says/because there sure isn't any place else/no
resource center/no library/no feminist counseling/no weekend
retreat/no place
where she's safe in america
or where she can forget
she's only alive
because when she was 8
her cousin was able to throw her into a ditch to hide
right before
he was grabbed & hung by the Ku Klux Klan

BY THE LIGHT

of the full moon I'm writing to you

here in this Grandmother whose silver hair

streaks the water leading to my heart

Wish you could feel this tide changing

Where does all the water go   Must be secret caves under

the ocean   Imagine a wonderful party

with different waters laughing admiring flirting

Ah Querida O you are such a strange & sinuous pretty green

Mais oui! The rocks I passed over today inspired me!

Language with no name my lips speak you

Nothing but water soothes

There's a FISH   Slaps the darkness

Too many lights on the far shore   on all night they're

a desecration   We're well-lit

longing for our deep black night mystery   where spirit is

Fear warps us   *O LOOK A SHHHHOOooootttting star*

red gold moving like a rainbow

Grandmother's silver braid rustles on the water

She's going dancing tonight

She'll burn the ground with her quick deer feet

O she's so moony in her shawl of stars   love, c

for Gloria Yamato

GOVERNMENT PEANUT BUTTER

There was a skin to bones cat living in Clyde's abandoned car
it went in & out through the broken windshield
The boys were torturing him & then we took over to save him   All
we had was white bread & government peanut butter which we hated
So did the cat   He would eat some & his eyes would bulge
like they were going to pop out & then he would look at us like
Are you serious
We thought maybe we could steal some cat food from stores
because they only watched the candy up front   So we rigged
a scheme where somebody would make a lot of fuss about which
candy bar to buy which was a lie because we all knew
to the last nut which candy bar was whose favorite
It was our serious business
I stole more than anybody because I was pretty good at getting
the little can up under my dress between my legs fast & then
going out like I was going to go to the bathroom at any minute
A skill I later used quite lucratively as a teenager in pursuit
of nail polish   face powder & sunglasses
We did a different store every time I must have learned
San Francisco running around stealing for that cat
For awhile he stayed in the basement of our building
which was a little warmer than Clyde's car & less likely
to have a drunk barge in on him to sleep
We called him Gus until Gus had kittens & then we didn't know
what to call him
They all died almost as soon as they were born   I stole a towel
from the Chinese laundry's line to bury them   digging their
grave at night through hard clay of the vacant lot next door
after I made dinner & cleaned the kitchen   My mother yelling
out the back window that I was as crazy as my goddamn Indian
grandfather & I was going to die in a nut house just like him
or get a terrible disease from those stupid kittens
which were so soft & sad   Gus disappeared afterward

I wondered if my mother got the pound to come get her & kill her
when I was in school because no one ever saw her at all ever
again not even her dead body in a garbage can which was strange
but I didn't dare ask & get a whipping
that peanut butter
could kill you

in memory of Blo

WINTER EVENING

in the northern mountains
Moon is a silver turtle
moving slowly through stars

for Marlene Wong

RICHARD WRIGHT I WISH YOU WERE HERE

it's 1987 I'm writing this on a paper bag at the quickie store
where we've stopped for lunch
& I noticed the home video cassette
for a fine movie made from your book   *Native Son*
which I'd like to see again even though we don't have a VCR
Make a tornado in your grave now
for 6 pictures on the cover of the box
5 of these are of white actors
one of whom I don't even remember
The one Black face   in a movie of Black life
is Oprah Winfrey who plays Bigger's mother
Victor Love   the star   the Native Son
is not pictured
even on the back   even tiny
I need you Richard Wright to stare at me across this formica table
our eyes flaming with indigestion & high blood pressure
nodding slowly as we murmur
Yeah   only in america
Yeah   the central character lands on the publicity floor
if he's a Black man
Richard Wright please shrug for me as I leave for work
where I could talk about this
watch the veils slide over their white eyes
Yeah   america

for Audre Lorde

INUIT SONGS

to soothe a crying baby   for the water   for wings of wind

Sisters   they sing to one another face to face

their mouths only a few inches away from each other

looking directly into one another's eyes

She wears an ivory baby carrier which their mother wore

to carry them

The first time you meet someone as strangers you throat sing

toying with her long fringe as she spoke

The men do drum dancing

Women are the smart ones & do the singing   she laughs

but he's written a song & she'll drum for him

A song about how bad he's been in his life & how good

He turns his back to the audience when he drums

dances as he calls   they're with each other   not us

the mixed audience of other Native Nations & whites

She sings a polar bear song which was her grandfather's

He says   *Nowadays nobody makes songs so we use the old ones*

of our parents   *This song*   *is one my father wrote*

about when the people were starving

the white woman on the other side of me

laughs

for Elizabeth Markell

90

LET ME TOUCH

like falling cherry petals your face
after you come circling in the stillness
our hearts like hummingbirds
let me sweet pink & tender kiss your breasts
your eyes closed softly in dreams of whirling stars
our bellies
wet & stuck

for BJ

HERBERT JOSEPH JEANS

died of AIDS, Oct. 31, 1987

Here are tears Sweet Man to wash you to the other side
up there in those glittering stars Hey   I know you're gonna be
so bright with your frosted blue pearl toenails & the longest
fingernails of any drag queen in the world
You Navajo/Oto hair burner with your pink scarf
& black alligator tote bag full of old beaded moccasins
jewelry   more silk scarves
I can hear you sashaying around up there   Hey Herbie
we'll miss you   Hey here's a thousand
yellow roses   you love so much   here's my hand
again   touching your forehead like a mother or sister to see
if your fever's worse   Sleeping next to you in my flannel gown
Oh the stars were wondering those nights
Hey we'll bead you a square for the AIDS quilt
Girl they'll never see   sewing like that again
cut crystal beads of yellow roses & your name in silver bugle beads
Hey Sweet Man every summer I'll paint
my toenails pearly blue to say hello
Do my very best to follow your advice
Hey Girl
Go out there & have a
GGGGGGGOOOOOOOOOOODDDDDD time

I COULD CARVE

these words in stones to leave on the moon or farther
Dark black smooth ones   Pink gray dappled beach granite
Green ones with white feather smoke lines   I could weave
your name through every muscle of my body black with longing to be
in
you   Have your mouth & fingers take me farther than the moon
dappled with colors I've seen only in my sleep while your body
prays beside mine through smooth nights   No more bones cocks
horses drag me in terror   These answers in your feather green
eyes   whose questions were dark until near a fire
at the beach you sat on a driftwood log   our eyes were one light
while the sun considered farther shores   You walked with me
as I carried buckets of salt water to douse forgotten flames
whose smoke I smell in my hair now as your hands
collect me carefully   sorting colors for smooth cloth
tied with feathers   My heart hears your voice   gallops
like black silk   You brush me   my muscles ripple dreams
Our smoky thighs dapple stars
I put my questions under stones   Lap you
in
Shores of desire drink me with new horses whose feet of smoke dance
on the moon weaving answers through every moment
Suns in our bellies as we dream of sleeping beside each other
until through a fire of years
we are no more than dust rolling itself into stones
Our fingers traced with granite where we've carved our bodies Our
in

for BJ Collins

GAY AMERICAN INDIANS MARCH ON
WASHINGTON, D.C.

My voice is a basket   calls   weave a hidden story with no
photographs through blue hours over america going home
from going where we weren't quite welcome   Going where I'm
greeted after 2 days with enthusiasm but not fed   He wept over
the phone at 7:30 a.m.   No one would take him in last night
I was clear across town & out to dinner after waiting 2 hours
for his call   in a strange city as all cities are strange
They threw him in the street   Finally someone else took him in
still crying   a relief bird   anger bird   panic bird
a 16 block walk with luggage bird   My voice weaves call
me a basket where her black eyes were closed maybe jealous who
knows   where hers were drunk belligerent ready to go to jail
in a haze of broken heart vomit & my lover's friend would only
let me stay there if I had sex with her
where someone else wanted to help but did nothing
where she was silent on the subject   where we weren't needed
or respected   where I was a grieving bird   where no one spoke
Menominee or had even heard of us not even the eye bird darting
for approval   Cut off in mid-sentence   No apology or one that
was an excuse   not from the heart   She spoke to me of her
desire for all others   bird who pecked until I bled
my eyes black with undreamt songs
A basket calls weave me into joy away from this bitter meat
turbulence of mistrust   engine trouble in the communications pit
elbowing for position bird   take all the credit & run bird
slapped down bird   nails not clean enough & lonely bird
queers in suits who spoke only to each other
huge groups of all white queers who didn't notice their
albino effect   Microphone removed in mid-poem they didn't want
to bother with me   Change hotel rooms 5 times in 7 days
eat popeye chicken with burning belly   Bird whose wings
tear with ignorance assumptions indifference   Tall white taking
bird   Big talking black bird   Narrow bird who leans
into your face   swallows all your breath
They say we're the same loins pulsing   but eyes dark with cold
unless we've got a Real Indian Souvenir to sell

94

gay white america same as straight white
Our black hair birds hurt going home
Looking for grass to weave through holes they leave us
cheering as we round the corner in the parade
to show they Love oh how they Love those Indians
Bird weaves a memory of 2 a.m.   Nowhere to go
My clothes locked up in a hotel room
where the boss has changed the key
familiar desperation   familiar brown bird arguing with white
assistant manager whose suit hissed demanding humiliation
Even in gay america   no place for Indian birds at the inn
a basket empty with promises   botched airline tickets
I whisper to a bird going by in the blues
she was right to refuse to come & eat indifference   rudeness
she knew what would be in the bowl   We should be grateful
they let us come at all or asked us to speak when they
could have had hours more of Jesse Jackson who didn't mention
Indians in his list of the deprived who should vote for him & isn't
even queer
Burnt basket we know so well
            Praying for thunder to clear the air

for Randy Burns

THREE

children, Pajuta, Skybird & Sherri expand
the world to a small pool
of slippery stones   cold spring water
inside an overhanging willow
where 2 swallows peck for bugs
as the wind comes up
my jeans hot   my fingers unravel
simple shouts of fear   exhilaration   challenge
they've forgotten me
as Skybird pitches a large rock in front of her
climbs to it   throws it forward again
to bring it home
Sherri leads the way while Pajuta
howls from a place where he's been stranded
we're safe in the river's breath
soft as their eyes
as grinning they get their clothes
all wet

WATER

She walked again over stones of so many colors listening to quiet
lapping   rustle of mallard wings as they drifted   high screams of
hungry gulls   Mountains were still there   could be relied on
And water   So often she'd come here with torn eyes   her heart
frantic   hands twisted in her pockets   head soggy with grief
asking to be healed   Another fight   long & miserable over the
telephone with accusations that didn't belong to them but to some
characters in a soap opera paid to say such things   She held
tenderness in memory   brief as flight   hands cupping her breasts
her own mouth nuzzling the softness of her lover   That made sense
like corn meal or potatoes or onions could be made useful   She had
these fights with white flowers   When brown flowers fought with
her it was about money or flirting in the bar or drinking too much or
sex   Fights like rocks   that ended   were concrete   not at all
mysterious   They were the fights she'd heard & watched all her life
But these others spoke to her as though across water   The sound
carried   was amplified   but the words were lost   indistinct
Often she'd say   *Please explain I don't know what you're talking about*
Their frustration with her would infuriate her further   Speaking
different languages they knew no sign   They fought about words
concepts   about all you couldn't see or grasp or cook with   They
wanted things from her that she could not give   She wanted to give
her hands loving cooking tending gathering   They wanted
something more which belonged only to sky   to earth   to first
buds of spring   They wanted her spirit to obey them   She
couldn't wear those kinds of shoes   She continued to love them
to kiss them   Easier because they were so many   Because brown
women often did not find her desirable   Because maybe her mystery
was no mystery to them   Because sometimes dark eyes looking into
dark eyes hurts too much   Because we've been brainwashed to see
only blonde as beautiful   Because there are so few of us that
friendship is safer & lasts   Because it is more comfortable to be
loved by those connected to those who run everything   White
flowers tended to stay   Driven by curiosity perhaps   They'd say
You fascinate me   What are you thinking   She might answer that she
was looking at the wild rose hips to see if they were ready to harvest
They'd answer in exasperation   *But what are you REALLY thinking*

She turned away not knowing what they meant   As soon describe how water flows as describe the quickly passing patterns of thoughts
     Talking to her for hours of their lives   their families   their opinions on everything   even about things they hadn't seen   She liked to listen to these stories of another country   Cautious about sharing her stories because she hated their pity or horror or thrilled gasps or not laughing in the right places   They often said she had a bizarre sense of humor   But she knew their hands & mouths were filled with love   *Communication* they said   *We have terrible communication*   She'd nod & go on slicing vegetables for dinner
She wanted so deeply to bridge that gap   to understand her fascination with that other world she mocked & hated & admired
She encouraged her friends to go to college though she could not face it herself   She wanted a place   It had to be here in this white world
She could not be a lesbian on the reservation especially since she had too many white ways
She wanted to be able to go to bars & laugh & clap women on the back & talk freely about jobs & television shows   She was one of them
She didn't like men in her bed   There was nothing to be done about that   Brown flowers came & went   Sometimes they called themselves players   which meant they couldn't take her seriously sometimes she wouldn't act right   Sometimes they said she was too close or too uppity or they said nothing & she thought they didn't care
Sometimes they hurt her so badly she left without speaking
Sometimes their drinking flooded her
Walking the beach she wanted to hold communication in her hand like a stone or shell   look at it closely until she understood
Somewhere in a place she rarely went   she knew   they were all underwater gasping   They all wanted to be of a place   to know each other as kin   to belong   but they didn't even eat the same foods   they came with armloads of other cultures who hated anyone unlike themselves   They could hardly find a clear place to speak
There would be meetings   coalitions   study groups   She would go   watch the arguments   desperation for power   anger   She would in turn be angry   desperate & arguing   Walking home she wondered how they'd ever make something of so much misunderstanding   She would see one woman chosen as scapegoat & beaten down   She had seen that so many times   She had done it once & still carried the shame   She could no longer go to meetings
She wanted to do something slowly   carefully   with respect

She wanted to know what it was that really needed to be done   She
wanted a new season with her whole being   Dreaming of it
awakening to this icy reality with groans in her heart   the longing
unbreakable in her chest   Not more bandaging   Not more
mopping up of blood & urine & grief   She wanted to sit for a long
long time with women not speaking   Until like stones they grew
used to one another & didn't need to fight   Didn't need to tear one
another apart to survive   Didn't need to play distorted ego games to
feel more powerful or more correct than anyone   She wanted to
walk backwards   She wanted the separations healed
She wanted to know where to go to make the best use of herself
She wanted to cook a feast that would bring all the women together
laughing   No one would look down on anyone else   Abuse of all
kinds would stop   She stood looking across the water watching the
light move as the afternoon went over the mountains in coral streaks
She remembered her father saying   *Ah little mitamu   you are such a
dreamer*

for Rosie Diaz

CEREMONY FOR COMPLETING A POETRY READING

This is a give away poem
You've come gathering   made a circle with me of the places
I've wandered   I give you   the first daffodil opening
from earth I've sown   I give you warm loaves of bread baked
in soft mounds like breasts   In this circle I pass each of you
a shell from our mother sea   Hold it in your spirit   Hear
the stories she'll tell you   I've wrapped your faces
around me   a warm robe   Let me give you ribbonwork leggings
dresses sewn with elk teeth   moccasins woven with red
& sky blue porcupine quills
I give you blankets woven of flowers & roots   Come closer
I have more to give   this basket is very large
I've stitched it of your kind words
Here is a necklace of feathers & bones
a sacred meal of chokecherries
Take this mask of bark which keeps out the evil ones
This basket is only the beginning
There is something in my arms for all of you
I offer this memory of sunrise seen through ice crystals
Here   an afternoon of looking into the sea from high rocks
Here   a red-tailed hawk circles over our heads
One of her feathers drops for your hair
May I give you this round stone which holds an ancient spirit
This stone will soothe you
Within this basket is something you've been looking for
all of your life   Come take it   Take as much as you need
I give you seeds of a new way
I give you the moon shining on a fire of singing women
I give you the sound of our feet dancing
I give you the sound of our thoughts flying
I give you the sound of peace moving into our faces & sitting down
Come   This is a give away poem
I cannot go home
until you have taken everything & the basket which held it
When my hands are empty
I will be full

ACKNOWLEDGMENTS

As nothing is possible without relationship, I wish to speak of those who've sustained me, given me lessons & shaped my visions. I thank my mother & father for bringing me here. My first woman lover, Peter, literally rescued me from the gutter—drugs & tricking—to love me for 8 years while I tried to kill myself; was in & out of looney bins & continued to sleep with men because I was afraid to call myself lesbian. Her courage & loyalty taught me my first scraps of self-esteem. I owe her my life.

When I was fresh from my last looney bin, Kate Millett encouraged me to publish. It was the first time anyone saw me as a writer instead of a nut & it's from that moment that I resolved to live, to stay out of bins & to be a voice for all of us who aren't supposed to speak. It's been more than ten years, but I've done it, & in her honor, I've included some prose, as she hates poetry.

I'm deeply grateful to Audre Lorde for her creative inspiration & for telling me to take myself seriously.

Barbara Cameron is the strong wind who brought my work to the attention of Gloria Anzaldúa. Barbara's patience through many years of my Scorpio rages & passions has been magnificent. Gloria has loved my work so much that I began to love it & to have the confidence that helps this book appear.

I've been inspired by the creative work of so many, among them, Dian Million, Elizabeth Woody, Lillian Pitt, Kim Anno, Beth Brant, Sharol Graves, Canyon Sam, Wendy Cadden, Jeanne Clark, Ann Hollingsworth, Laura Israel, Carole Graham, Nanci Stern, Paula Ross, Marcy Alaincraig, Sarita Johnson, Theresa Clark, Carletta Wilson, Gloria Yamato, Cheryl Harrison, Gwen Avery, Blackberri, Frieda Feen, Jackie Moorey, Karin Spitfire, Ana R. Kissed, Mary McGough, Joy Harjo, R. Carlos Nakai, Mary Watkins, Susana Santos, John Trudell, Floyd Westerman, Kitaro & many others.

A very special thanks to my three cats—Beast, who sleeps in my hair at night; Sappho who is a spry 14 & especially, Pusiina, who perched on my neck most of the time I typed this.

My deepest thanks to Gay American Indians, which has been a huge source of pride & strength, especially to Marlyn, Gary, Clyde, Trini, Jerry, Will & Randy.

I've been blessed with love from many sources, often unexpectedly. For all those who have encouraged me, given me gifts after readings & wept at my words, I pray that you will also speak out until our voices drown out Warmaker (Trudell's word).

I'm very grateful to Press Gang Publishers for all their work, despite difficulties, their patience with my year long procrastination, especially to Della McCreary who called & wrote & called with encouragement when I was convinced this was a waste of trees. Barbara Kuhne is the one who helped me figure out how to have it look the way I speak it & re-think my line breaks, which were too long to fit. Penny Goldsmith survived typesetting this very complicated manuscript with sensitive & flying colors. I appreciate the generosity of my translators Juanita Ramos and Margarita Sewerin. Val Speidel was very helpful in negotiating the cover and layout terrain. Please join with me in thanking the women of the printing collective whose labor brings this book to your hands.

Some of my good friends are here, in various poems dedicated to them. They all know how much they are my breath of life, especially Valerie Street, who has known me longer than I can remember & is the only person I know who is better at intimidating fools than myself. Barbara Cameron, Co-Founder of GAI, is a cherished friend, even though I never write. A special thanks to Janis Portal for many years of friendship.

I hope all those I've lost touch with over the years, especially Leslie Dilbeck, Suzanne Cameron, Maria Leon, Terry Sanders, Kenya Johnson & Pam Hom will write to say Hey.

The Lesbians of Color Potluck keeps me as sane as it is possible to be (not all members would agree). Especially precious are the friendships of Gloria, Cheryl, Aisha, Jackie, Damita, Sky, Shirley, Rosie, Marlene, Celeste, Amanda, Dian, Viv, Theresa & Renée. Thanks also to our "white girls' auxillary" (this is a joke), Leslie, Barbara & BJ.

& so I come to you, BJ Collins, who has managed to love me for the last three years, sometimes by the skin of both our teeth. Wee Dew.

If anyone sees Joanne Garrett fooling around, better tell her to get on up here for a visit because the salmon are yelling her name.

I would like to honor the name of Ada Deer, who worked so hard for the re-instatement of my tribe & to honor all those with whom